Dinosaurs

Archaeopteryx

by Julie Murray

Dash!
LEVELED READERS
An Imprint of Abdo Zoom • abdobooks.com
1

Dash!
LEVELED READERS

Level 1 – Beginning
Short and simple sentences with familiar words or patterns for children who are beginning to understand how letters and sounds go together.

Level 2 – Emerging
Longer words and sentences with more complex language patterns for readers who are practicing common words and letter sounds.

Level 3 – Transitional
More developed language and vocabulary for readers who are becoming more independent.

THIS BOOK CONTAINS
RECYCLED MATERIALS

abdobooks.com

Published by Abdo Zoom, a division of ABDO, PO Box 398166, Minneapolis, Minnesota 55439.
Copyright © 2020 by Abdo Consulting Group, Inc. International copyrights reserved in all countries.
No part of this book may be reproduced in any form without written permission from the publisher.
Dash!™ is a trademark and logo of Abdo Zoom.

Printed in the United States of America, North Mankato, Minnesota.
052019
092019

Photo Credits: Alamy, Getty Images, Science Source, Shutterstock
Production Contributors: Kenny Abdo, Jennie Forsberg, Grace Hansen, John Hansen
Design Contributors: Dorothy Toth, Neil Klinepier

Library of Congress Control Number: 2018963181

Publisher's Cataloging in Publication Data

Names: Murray, Julie, author.
Title: Archaeopteryx / by Julie Murray.
Description: Minneapolis, Minnesota : Abdo Zoom, 2020 | Series: Dinosaurs |
   Includes online resources and index.
Identifiers: ISBN 9781532127168 (lib. bdg.) | ISBN 9781532128141 (ebook) |
   ISBN 9781532128639 (Read-to-me ebook)
Subjects: LCSH: Archaeopteryx--Juvenile literature. | Dinosaurs--Juvenile
   literature. | Dinosaurs--Behavior--Juvenile literature.
Classification: DDC 567.918--dc23

Table of Contents

Archaeopteryx

Was the Archaeopteryx a dinosaur? Was it a bird? It was both!

It had wings and feathers like a bird. Its head, hands, and tail were all like a dinosaur's.

It lived about 150 million years ago.

It was small. It was 1.6 feet (.49 m) long. It weighed only about 2 pounds (.91 kg).

It had wide wings, but it did not fly. It **glided** from tree to tree.

It had fingers with claws. These helped it climb trees. It had a long **snout**. Its teeth were tiny and sharp.

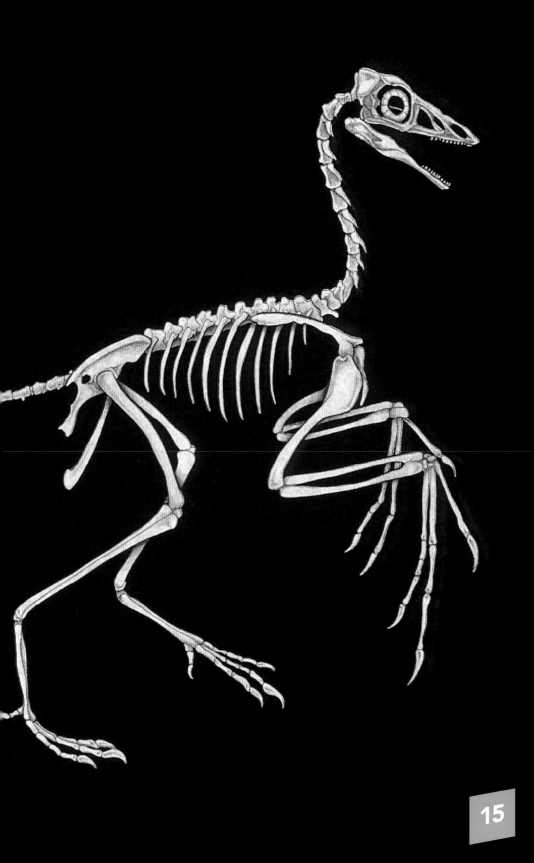

Its body was covered in feathers. It had a long, bony tail. Its legs were strong and it could run fast.

It likely ate small reptiles and mammals. It also probably ate insects.

Its **fossils** were first discovered in about 1860 in Germany.

More Facts

- Archaeopteryx is the oldest bird-like animal known.

- Its **fossils** were first found by a **paleontologist** named Hermann von Meyer.

- It had a special toe, like our thumb. This helped it hold onto things.

Glossary

fossil – the remains or trace of a living animal or plant from a long time ago. Fossils are found embedded in earth or rock.

glide – to move smoothly and continuously along without effort.

paleontologist – a scientist who studies fossils.

snout – the front part of an animal's head that sticks out and includes the nose, mouth, and jaws.

Index

Online Resources

Booklinks
NONFICTION NETWORK
FREE! ONLINE NONFICTION RESOURCES

To learn more about the Archaeopteryx, please visit **abdobooklinks.com** or scan this QR code. These links are routinely monitored and updated to provide the most current information available.